POEMS A

SUMMER

by
Mary
Fleeson

Early in the morning, Jesus stood on the shore,
but the disciples did not realize that it was Jesus.

He called out to them,
"Friends, haven't you any fish?"

"No," they answered.

He said, "Throw your
net on the right side
of the boat and you
will find some."
When they did,
they were unable
to haul the net
in because
of the large
number of fish.

John 21:4-6

Many times I have called on You,
sometimes in despair, sometimes in anger,
sometimes trying to hold the final straw away
from my aching back,
sometimes holding on to that rock-heavy burden
like it's a treasure,
sometimes I've felt like I was shouting at the wind...
And yet, when I stop my calling, shouting,
panic-induced over-thinking,
I have heard Your reply in the soft breeze
and the gentle wave,
"Trust Me, I am with you."
And I find, in time, that there is another way.

FOR EVER SINCE THE WORLD WAS CREATED,
PEOPLE HAVE SEEN THE EARTH AND SKY.
THROUGH EVERYTHING GOD MADE, THEY
CAN CLEARLY SEE HIS INVISIBLE QUALITIES -
HIS ETERNAL POWER AND DIVINE NATURE.

ROMANS 1:20

Spring morphs into Summer...

Days are long and sunshine-bright,

Nights are sticky-warm and sleep-deprived.

Pollen-filled air and bar-be-que wishes,

Birdsong fills the ear, red-velvet sunset fills the eye,

Long walks and cut grass scents.

Ozone wafts from high tide abandoned seaweed,

Glinting sea glass and worn-out shells await new purpose.

And I breathe deeply and give thanks.

Midsummer sky,
Forget Me Not blue with soaring birds
and sounds of the season.
The imperfect memories
of perfect Summers
of time gone by,
jostle to compare to today.

It was hotter then. It was colder then.

Midsummer night sky,
hardly dark, vast canopy of scudding clouds
and tiny twinkling balls of gas.
The perfect time
to contemplate life,
love, eternity, hope,
and faith in the Creator.

It was hotter then. It was colder then.

Sand between my toes,
Salty sea splashing, soothing my soul.
Dream-filled hours in the sun.

I know for sure that
my troubles, doubts and fears haven't disappeared
but for now,
I'll let them drift away on a seaweed scented breeze.

And I'll surrender too
my need to know, and control-freak tendencies
and for now,
I'll let the sun warm me like a hug of pure love.

HOW PRECIOUS TO ME ARE
YOUR THOUGHTS, GOD! HOW
VAST IS THE SUM OF THEM!
WERE I TO COUNT THEM,
THEY WOULD OUTNUMBER
THE GRAINS OF SAND -
WHEN I AWAKE, I AM STILL
WITH YOU.   PSALM 139:17-18

Your voice in the crashing wave and the howling wind,
'Follow Me!'
Your face in the clouds and the grains of sand,
'Trust Me!'
Your touch in the warm sun and the soft Summer rain,
'I am here.'

Little Brother,
Your eyes seem to see
with the wisdom of ages.
A wistful gaze
I wonder what you remember.

Clown Of The Sea,
Your colours so bright
you make me laugh,
then wistfully smile.
Do you know your charm?

I see Your wisdom
Creator God,
In the eyes of Your creations.
I see Your compassion
Creator God,
In the faces of Your children.

Puffins are also known as 'sea clowns' for their facial hues
and 'Fratercula Arctica' or 'Little brothers of the North' for
the monk-like colour and pattern of their plumage.

CREATOR AND THE
GOD **SEA**
YOU MADE AND EVERY
THE HEAVEN **THING**
AND THE THAT IS
EARTH IN THEM

And Summer sunlight falls bright on the distant shore,
Grass-green slopes and pastoral scenes.
Look further.
A steel grey river flowing painted carriers of people-kind,
Huddles of homes in accessible places.
Look further
Cities alive, bursting with potential,
Collecting excitement, distracting, beguiling.
Look further.
Nations creating, burying, reshaping,
Discovering place in the now of today.
Look further.
A world on the edge, it was always this fragile,
Help us to follow Your way.

And Summer starlight twinkles on the rippling waves,
Jewels scattered marking treasures to find.
Look deeper.
Within and without are strands of connection,
Knots of influence, compassion and care.
Look deeper.
Life, often waiting, longs to begin,
The whens and the ifs wistfully calling.
Look deeper.
Soul crying 'save me', heart saying 'love me',
Mind often doubting that anything is real.
Look deeper.
On the edge, I was always this fragile,
Help me to follow Your way.

As the waters move with the wind,
Let me be moved by Your Holy wind.
As the deep waters shelter life,
Let my deepest desire be to nurture others.
As the waves embrace the shore,
Let me embrace Your call.

I was paddling on the shore when I heard a voice say 'go deeper, the cool, soft, water of My love will soothe you, 'Go deeper' into My presence. I went in up to my knees and said, 'enough'. And the voice said, 'Hold My hand'.

May the God of hope fill you with all joy and peace as you trust in him, so that you may overflow with hope by the power of the Holy Spirit.

Romans 15:13

Sometimes I envy the birds
Clothed in soft beauty,
Not fearing the heights,
Gliding on unseen thermals,
Seeing a different viewpoint.
Sometimes I wish
That worry wasn't a word,
That fear didn't exist,
That faith was easy,
That I could see through other eyes...

...imagine...

Help me Loving God
to care enough to listen,
to be curious enough to look,
to be selfless enough to take action.

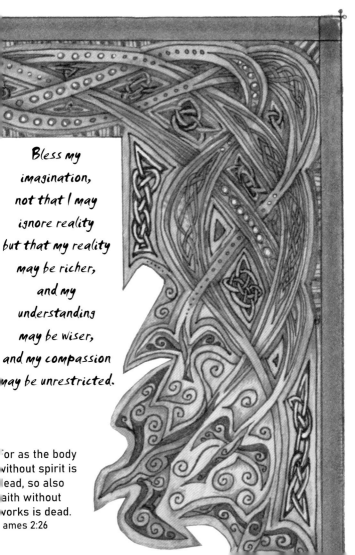

Bless my
imagination,
not that I may
ignore reality
but that my reality
may be richer,
and my
understanding
may be wiser,
and my compassion
may be unrestricted.

For as the body
without spirit is
dead, so also
faith without
works is dead.
James 2:26

Floundered
Failed
Cried
Wailed
Stepped
Tried

Grant
Grace
Wisdom
Passion
Love
Peace

Waiting
Watching
Anticipatin.
Wondering
Hoping
Praying